D1237855

VOLUME ONE: RISE OF THE VAMPIRES

THE CHRONICLES OF LEGION

FABIEN NURY

MATHIEU LAUFFRAU

MARIO ALBERTI

ZHANG XIAOYU

TIRSO

THE CHRONICLES OF LEGION

VOLUME ONE: RISE OF THE VAMPIRES

WRITTEN BY
FABIEN NURY

ART BY
MATHIEU LAUFFRAY
PAGES 3-13

MARIO ALBERTI
PAGES 14-25 AND 43-56

ZHANG XIAOYU
PAGES 26-40

TIRSO
PAGES 44-55
COLORS BY: JAVIER MARTIN

COVER ART BY
MATHIEU LAUFFRAY

TRANSLATED BY
VIRGINIE SELAVY

LETTERING BY
GABRIELA HOUSTON

What did you think of this book?
We love to hear from our readers. Please email us at:
readercomments@titanemail.com, or write to us at the above address.

To receive news, competitions, and exclusive offers online, please sign up for the Titan Comics newsletter on our website:
www.titan-comics.com

Follow us on Twitter
@ComicsTitan

Visit us at
facebook.com/comicstitan

The Chronicles of Legion: Rise of the Vampires
ISBN: 9781782760931

Published by Titan Comics
A division of Titan Publishing Group Ltd.
144 Southwark St. London SE1 0UP

A CIP catalogue record for this title is available from the British Library.
First edition: December 2014
Originally published in 2011 by Éditions Glénat, France as Les Chroniques de Legion: Livre 1

10 9 8 7 6 5 4 3 2 1

Printed in China.
Titan Comics. TC0193

HURRAH!
VICTORY!
THE TYRANT IS DEAD!!
GLORY TO THE SULTAN!
VICTORY!
VICTORY!
HURRAH!
LONG LIVE THE SULTAN!
TRANSYLVANIA, DECEMBER 14TH, 1476

VICTORY!
THE TYRANT IS DEAD!
WHERE IS HE?!
WHERE IS MY BROTHER?!

HE DIED LIKE A COWARD... THE COMMANDER OF THE SULTAN'S GUARD FOUND HIM HIDING AMONG HIS COURTESANS!
SELIM BEY MADE HIM KNEEL DOWN AND THEN HE CUT HIS DAMNED HEAD OFF!
MY BROTHER KNELT DOWN!?
DO YOU IMAGINE YOU CAN IMPRESS ME WITH YOUR BRAGGING, FOOL? WHAT YOU SAY IS IMPOSSIBLE! THERE IS NO ONE IN THIS WORLD WHO CAN FORCE VLAD TEPES TO KNEEL!
WHO WAS WITH HIM WHEN HE DIED?!
WHO WAS WITH MY BROTHER?

YOU WERE HIS FAVORITE -- I CAN TELL... THE MOST **BEAUTIFUL** OF ALL HIS CONCUBINES.
EVEN FACING DEATH, HE CHOSE TO COME TO YOU.
SO WHAT DO YOU FEEL NOW? NOW THAT YOUR KING IS DEAD?
DO YOU FEEL **SADNESS**?

OR **RELIEF**?...

WHY DELAY WHAT WE BOTH KNOW COMES **NEXT**? BELIEVE ME WHEN I SAY THAT I CAN'T WAIT FOR IT TO BE **OVER**...

NO...
AND WHAT DO YOU FEEL NOW, SELIM BEY?
PLEASURE?
OR TERROR...?

SELIM BEY, SHOW YOURSELF!
HURRY UP, MEN! BREAK THE DOOR DOWN!
KRAK!!
NO... NOT AGAIN...
NOT YET.
MEN! CALL THE GUARDS! SURROUND THE VILLAGE!
DON'T LET SELIM BEY ESCAPE!
FIND HIM!

HEH FINALLY...
AFTER A REIGN OF 17 YEARS, VLAD TEPES HAS FINALLY BEEN OVERCOME.
TELL ME, SELIM, DID HE DIE BRAVELY? DID HE SHOW DIGNITY IN HIS FINAL MOMENTS? WHEN HE WAS ALIVE, EVERYONE ALWAYS PRAISED HIS COURAGE. AND DREADED HIS CRUELTY... EVEN I ADMIRED HIM IN A WAY...
HOW A MAN DIES IS OF LITTLE IMPORTANCE. HE'S DEAD NOW -- THAT'S ALL THAT MATTERS. WHAT WILL HAPPEN TO RADU?
WHAT DO YOU THINK? HOW DO I ALWAYS DEAL WITH TRAITORS?
HE REBELLED AGAINST HIS OWN COMMANDER. BESIDES, NOW THAT HIS BROTHER IS DEAD, RADU'S OUTLIVED HIS USEFULENESS...
BUT YOU, SELIM BEY, YOU HAVE NOTHING OF A TRAITOR IN YOU. YOU'RE MY MOST LOYAL, AND MOST NOBLE WARRIOR.
AND TODAY YOU BRING ME THE MOST GLORIOUS OF ALL MY VICTORIES...
...HOW CAN I REWARD YOU?
I'VE ALREADY RECEIVED MY REWARD.
WELL BEYOND WEALTH...
...WELL BEYOND GLORY...

...I'VE BEEN GIVEN AN ETERNITY.

I TOLD THEM ABOUT MY BROTHER'S POWER.
THEY DIDN'T BELIEVE ME.
I WARNED THEM.
AND NOW IT'S TOO LATE. THEY BLAME ME FOR THE DEATH OF THEIR SULTAN.
THEY'RE PLANNING TO EXECUTE ME -- ME, RADU -- LIKE SOME COMMON TRAITOR.
IDIOTS...
DO THEY REALLY BELIEVE THAT MY BROTHER IS THE ONLY ONE OF HIS SPECIES?

SOMEWHERE ON THE ATLANTIC, 9TH MARCH 1521.
THE OCEAN IS RAGING IN FRONT OF ME. THE GALLEON THAT IS CARRYING US SEEMS SO FRAIL IN THE FACE OF SUCH RAW POWER. THE SMALLEST OF THESE WAVES COULD SWALLOW IT UP, AND YET...
...FOR FIVE WEEKS NOW, INDIFFERENT TO THE ANGER OF THE SEA, WE HAVE BEEN SAILING TOWARDS THE NEW WORLD.
CARLOS, MY FAITHFUL SERVANT, IS WORRIED. HE'D LIKE ME TO GO BACK TO MY CABIN. I TELL HIM TO BE QUIET.
I DON'T NEED TO OPEN MY LIPS TO GIVE HIM THIS ORDER...

MY THOUGHTS TRAVEL ACROSS SPACE AND TIME... THEY SAIL IN THE MULTITUDE OF MY MEMORIES... THEY SUMMON NAMES, FACES...
...AND, WITHOUT REALLY KNOWING WHY, THEY BECOME FIXED ON SELIM BEY.
I'M WAITING. I'M WAITING FOR THIS STRANGE LAND TO FINALLY APPEAR IN FRONT OF US... I'M WAITING TO STEP ONTO THIS VIRGIN CONTINENT THAT WILL SOON BE MINE.
I'M WAITING, AND, AS I WAIT, I DREAM...
OF ALL MY INCARNATIONS, HE WAS CERTAINLY ONE OF THE MOST PLEASING. HE WAS STRONG, INTELLIGENT, MERCILESS... HE KNEW HOW TO ENJOY THE SIMPLE PLEASURES OF LIFE.

WITH THE SULTAN'S BLOOD STILL WET ON HIS HANDS AND THE OTTOMANS HOT ON HIS HEELS, SELIM BAY REACHED THE BLACK SEA.
THERE, HAVING NEVER ONCE STOOD ON A DECK, RIGGED A SAIL OR FLOGGED A SAILOR, HE CHOSE A LIFE OF PIRACY.
HE WAS A NATURAL. ONE, THEN TWO, THEN TEN SHIPS FELL TO HIS PREDATIONS ABOUT THE INNER SEA. GREAT WEALTH AND CONQUESTS WERE HIS.
LADEN WITH RICHES, HE RETIRED TO AN OPPULENT HOME IN GRANADA, LIVING IN LUXURY FOR 15 YEARS.
HIS ONLY COMPANION WAS DON VICTORIO DE LA FUENTE. CAPTURED ABOARD SALIM'S GALLEON, VICTOR WAS A HOSTAGE TURNED CONFIDANT, AND WAS THE FATHER OF MY PRESENT INCARNATION.
SELIM BEY AND HIS HOSTAGE OFTEN PLAYED CHESS. SELIM BEY WOULD ALWAYS WIN, OF COURSE...
...BUT THEIR LAST GAME REMAINED UNFINISHED. IT WAS IN JANUARY 14

GRANADA FELL, BRINGING AN END TO THE REIGN OF THE MOORS...
...AND, AS THE CITY FELL, SO DID THE LEGENDARY SELIM BEY.
THE NATURE OF THAT FALL REMAINS SHROUDED IN MYSTERY.
CRUSADERS FOUND HIS BLOOD-SOAKED CORPSE ON THE STEPS OF HIS PALACE, HAVING APPARENTLY FALLEN VICTIM TO HIS ERSTWHILE HOSTAGE.
WHETHER IT WAS THE TRUTH OR NOT, VICTORIO DE LA FUENTE WAS ONCE MORE FREE.
AND SPAIN REJOICED. ITS NOBLE SON WAS NOW A HERO, A NEW AND BLESSED CAMPEADOR REUNITED WITH HIS FAMILY...

HAVE BEEN GONE 15 YEARS BUT
, DONA, KNEW HER BELOVED WELL
H TO KNOW THAT THE MAN WHO
RNED WAS NOT HER HUSBAND.
THAT HE WAS NOW UNBEATABLE AT CHESS WAS ATTRIBUTED TO TIME WELL SPENT WHILST IN CAPTIVITY.
THE MARK ON THE BACK OF HIS NECK? A SLAVER'S BRAND, NOTHING MORE. IN TRUTH IT WAS A MARK SELIM BEY'S MISTRESSES WOULD HAVE RECOGNIZED. ASSUMING THEY HAD LIVED THAT LONG...
HIS COMPADRES SAW NOTHING BUT THEIR OLD FRIEND. YET POOR DONA SAW A CUCKOO IN THE NEST... SHE RAVED, WHILE THOSE AROUND HER SHOCK THEIR HEADS SADLY.
HOCK OF HIS
SAID, PITIABLY.
ER MAD. SHE WAS
TO A CONVENT,
HEARTBROKEN
A GOOD AND
LE CHRISTIAN,
IS TIME TO HIS
EDUCATION.
IS VIRTOUS LIFE WAS LONG AND FULL OF GRACE.
REPARING HIS SOUL TO MEET GOD, HE ASKED TO
EAK TO THE MOST BEAUTIFUL OF HIS DAUGHTERS
ONE LAST TIME...
...GABRIELLA.

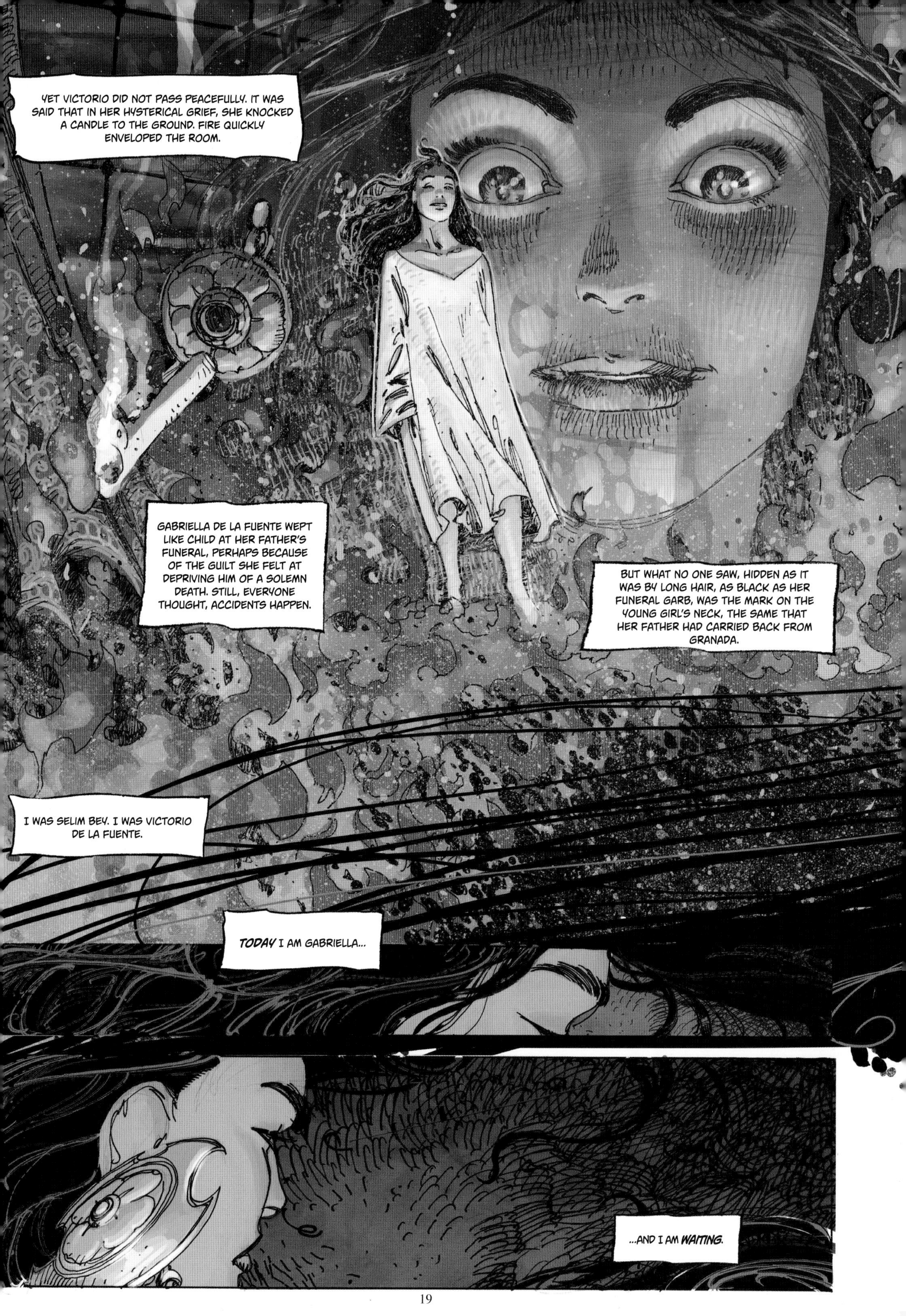
YET VICTORIO DID NOT PASS PEACEFULLY. IT WAS SAID THAT IN HER HYSTERICAL GRIEF, SHE KNOCKED A CANDLE TO THE GROUND. FIRE QUICKLY ENVELOPED THE ROOM.
GABRIELLA DE LA FUENTE WEPT LIKE CHILD AT HER FATHER'S FUNERAL, PERHAPS BECAUSE OF THE GUILT SHE FELT AT DEPRIVING HIM OF A SOLEMN DEATH. STILL, EVERYONE THOUGHT, ACCIDENTS HAPPEN.
BUT WHAT NO ONE SAW, HIDDEN AS IT WAS BY LONG HAIR, AS BLACK AS HER FUNERAL GARB, WAS THE MARK ON THE YOUNG GIRL'S NECK, THE SAME THAT HER FATHER HAD CARRIED BACK FROM GRANADA.
I WAS SELIM BEY. I WAS VICTORIO DE LA FUENTE.
TODAY I AM GABRIELLA...
...AND I AM WAITING.

DONA GABRIELLA, FOR HEAVEN'S SAKE, GET INSIDE RIGHT THIS MINUTE!
HERNAN TORRES WOULD HAVE US ALL EXECUTED IF YOU WERE TO FALL ILL BEFORE WE REACHED THE SHORE.

DO NOT WORRY, CAPTAIN, I HAVE AN IRON CONSTITUTION.

ARE YOU CERTAIN YOU WOULDN'T BE MORE COMFORTABLE IN YOUR CABIN? IT WOULD GIVE YOU A CHANCE TO GET READY BEFORE WE ARRIVE...

YOU DOUBT MY BEAUTY, CAPTAIN? DO YOU THINK THAT I NEED TO PRIMP AND PREEN TO MAKE MYSELF ATTRACTIVE?

ER, NO... OF COURSE NOT. I JUST MEANT...

WAS I NOT SELECTED FROM THE MOST BEAUTIFUL FLOWERS OF SPANISH ARISTOCRACY TO MARRY THE FAMOUS CONQUISTADOR HERNAN TORRES? DID TORRES HIMSELF NOT EQUIP THIS SHIP ESPECIALLY SO THAT I COULD JOIN HIM?

STILL, THIS IS NOT YOUR PLACE. PLEASE RETURN TO YOUR CABIN.

NO, I **DON'T** THINK I SHALL. AND YOU CAN HARDLY FORCE ME. WHAT WILL YOU **DO**, YOUR GRACE? **CRUCIFY** ME? BURN ME ON A STAKE FOR DISOBEYING YOU? I AM NOT ONE OF THOSE COWS YOU BRING OUT OF THE HOLD ONLY AFTER WE HAVE REACHED THE PORT.

CAPTAIN, YOU TOLD ME YOURSELF THAT WE'LL BE THERE IN JUST A FEW HOURS... UNLESS, OF COURSE, YOU MADE A **MISTAKE** IN YOUR CALCULATIONS?
NO, I... **OF COURSE** NOT!

WELL, THAT'S PERFECT THEN. SEEING AS THE NEW WORLD IS SO CLOSE, IT IS ONLY **FITTING** THAT I'M HERE TO S--

LAND AHEAD!

LAND DEAD AHEAD!

...SEE IT.

WHO IS THAT?
MARTIN, HERNAN TORRES'S SON. HIS BASTARD SON, THAT IS. HIS MOTHER WAS A NATIVE. DON'T WORRY, DONA GABRIELLA, HE HAS NO RIGHT TO HIS FATHER'S FORTUNE.

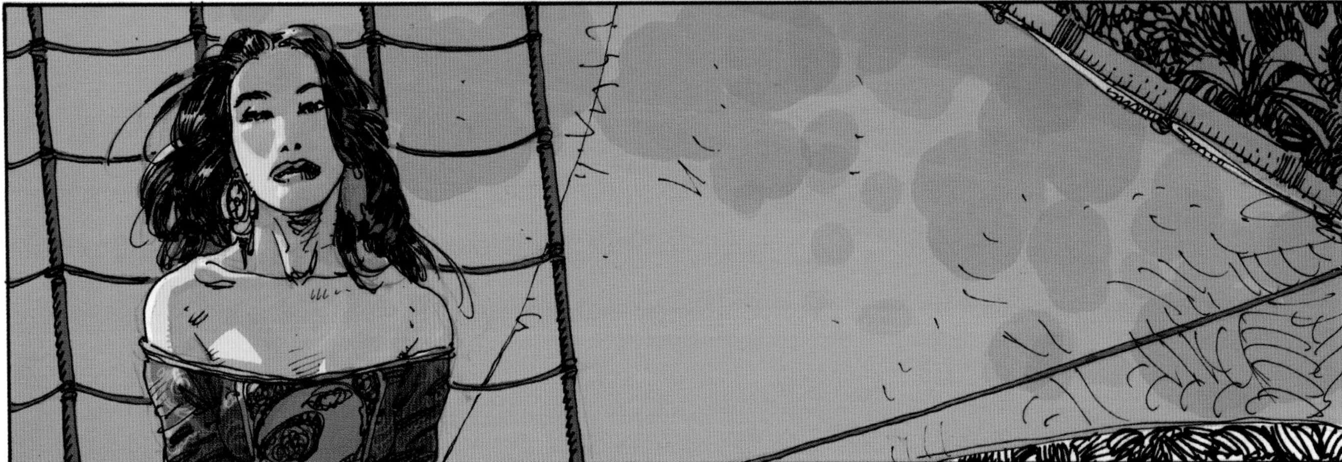

MARTIN...

I'M ALIVE. I'M FREE.

I MUST THINK, ALWAYS THINK, NOT FORGET WHO I AM.

HERE ARE MY PEOPLE, HERE ARE MY SUBJECTS. THEY SMELL ME, THEY TOUCH ME...

...I LET THEM TASTE MY BLOOD, SO THAT EACH OF THEM COMES UNDER MY CONTROL. I SPREAD MYSELF OUT, I MULTIPLY...

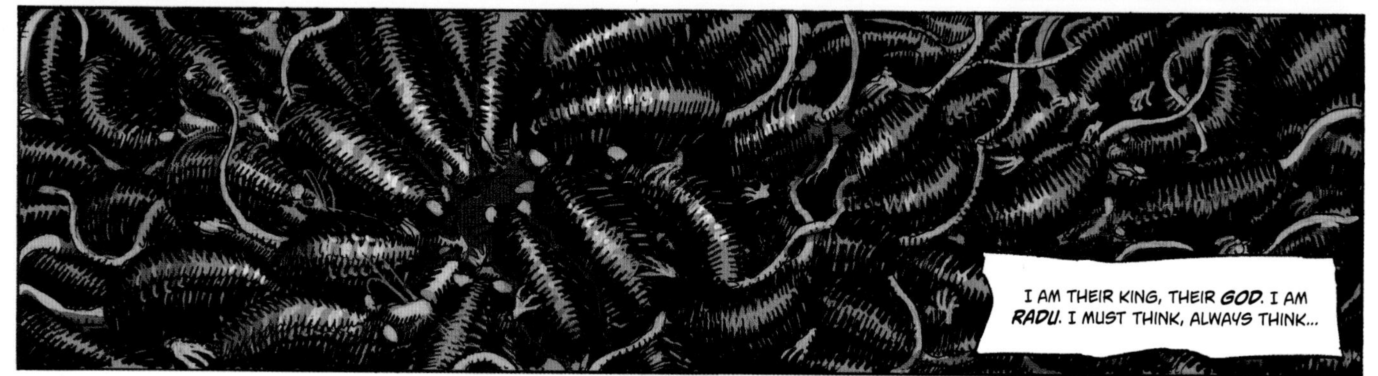
I AM THEIR KING, THEIR GOD. I AM RADU. I MUST THINK, ALWAYS THINK...

RUSSIA, 27TH NOVEMBER 1812.

I'M COLD. MY HANDS FEEL NUMB.
I LIKE IT.

I'M SCARED. MY LEGS CAN BARELY CARRY ME. I LOVE IT.

NOTHING LIKE A GOOD WAR...

...TO MAKE YOU FEEL ALIVE.

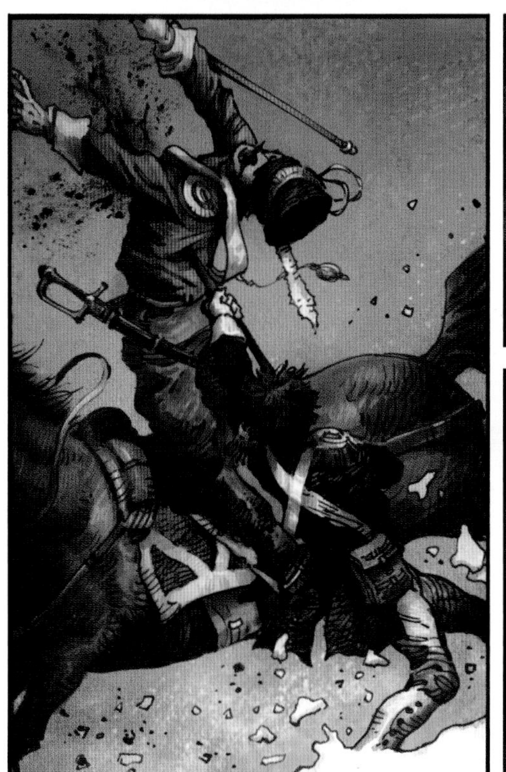

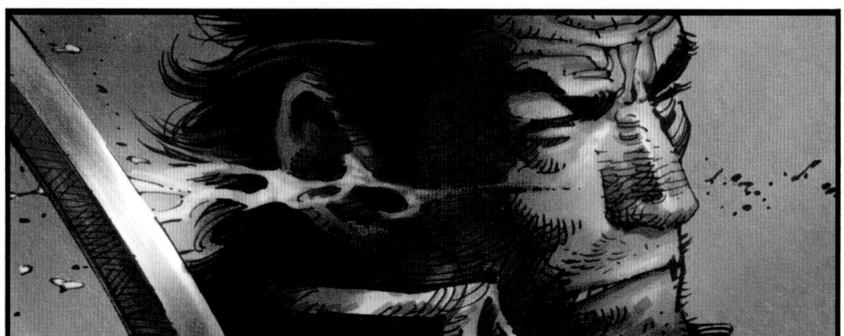

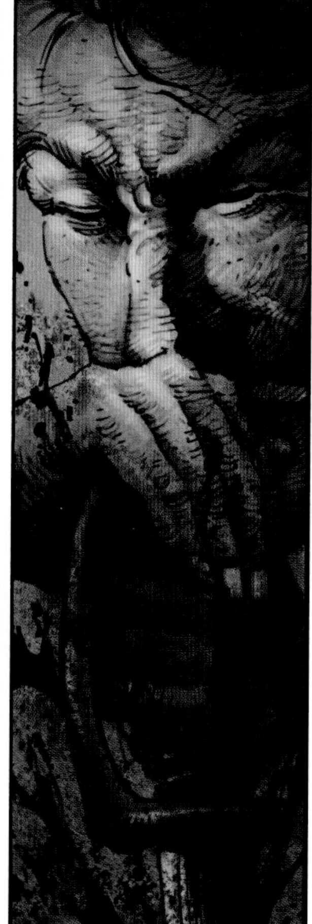

AND JUST LIKE THAT -- IT'S OVER. ANOTHER **GLORIOUS VICTORY** FOR **ARMAND MALACHIE**, THE HUSSAR CAPTAIN.
I TAKE THE TIME TO COUNT MY MEN.

KHOLYA.
STERN.
HARTMANN.
THE ELDER FERAUD BROTHER.

THE ONLY ONE MISSING IS...

...GABRIEL?

I CAN'T WALK, CAPTAIN... I CAN'T...

YOU'VE BEEN HIT IN THE STOMACH, GABRIEL.

NO! I... I CAN CARRY HIM! I CAN TAKE HIM BACK TO THE CAMP. I CAN--

ALL YOU'LL MANAGE TO DO IS TO MAKE HIM SUFFER POINTLESSLY. MOVE AWAY, FERAUD.
NO! I WON'T LET YOU DO THIS!

I MUST DO IT. WOULD YOU RATHER HE FELL INTO THE HANDS OF THE COSSACKS? OR SHOULD WE LEAVE HIM TO SUFFER ALONE IN THE COLD FOR HOURS?
YOU WOULDN'T DO THIS IF HE WERE YOUR BROTHER!

IF HE WERE MY OWN BROTHER, I'D KILL HIM MYSELF. IS THAT WHAT YOU WANT? CAN YOU DO IT?

DON'T COME ANY CLOSER! DON'T--

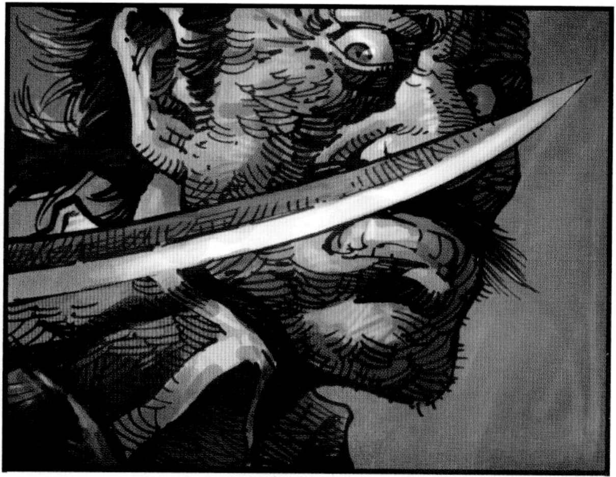

THE CAPTAIN GAVE YOU AN ORDER.
BRAVE KHOLYA. THE MOST LOYAL OF MY MEN. HE'D FOLLOW ME TO HELL IF I ASKED HIM TO.

DON'T BE ANGRY WITH THE CAPTAIN, BROTHER. YOU KNOW HE'S JUST DOING WHAT HE'S GOTTA DO, SAME AS ALWAYS...

HOW OLD ARE YOU, GABRIEL?
19, CAPTAIN. AND... AND YOU?

I'M OLDER, GABRIEL. OLDER THAN YOU CAN IMAGINE.

IS THERE... IS THERE SOMETHING... ...AFTER?

I DON'T KNOW. THERE ARE THINGS THAT EVEN *I* DON'T KNOW...

I DON'T **BELIEVE** YOU... YOU ALWAYS KNOW EVERYTHING ABOUT EV--

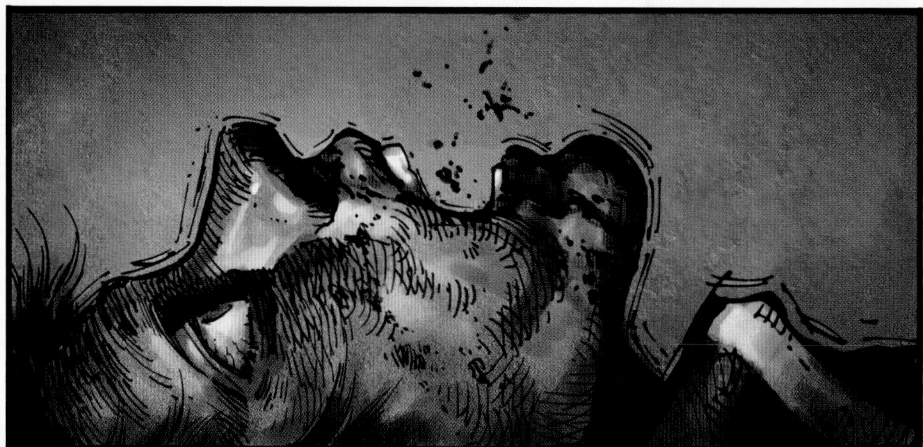

IT'S *DONE*.

KHOLYA, YOU CAN LET FERAUD GO NOW. HE WON'T DO ANYTHING. HE KNOWS IT HAD TO BE DONE.

YOU HAVE TEN MINUTES TO BURY HIM. MEET US AT THE TOP OF THE HILL.

CAPTAIN?

I THANK YOU... IN HIS MOTHER'S NAME.

I TAKE THEM TO THE TOP. THEY DON'T UNDERSTAND WHY, BUT THEY'RE SOLDIERS AND USED TO FOLLOWING ORDERS WITHOUT QUESTION.

WE ARE LIVING THROUGH A CRUCIAL MOMENT IN HISTORY, BUT I FEEL LIKE I'M THE ONLY ONE WHO TRULY COMPREHENDS ITS MEANING... I DON'T WANT TO MISS THIS SPECTACLE...

TODAY, AFTER 12 YEARS OF CONSTANT WAR, THE GREAT CONQUEROR FACES DEFEAT. IT'S A FEELING THAT I HAVE KNOWN MYSELF.
I KNOW THAT LESS THAN BARELY A LEAGUE FROM HERE, THE EMPEROR IS CONTEMPLATING THE SAME VIEW. I KNOW HIM WELL. I'VE BEEN FOLLOWING HIM FOR EIGHT YEARS. I'VE BEEN ALONE WITH HIM. I COULD HAVE BECOME THIS MAN, IF I WANTED, AND MADE HISTORY IN HIS PLACE... BUT I PREFER MINE. BETTER TO FIGHT THAN REIGN.

HE KNOWS, LIKE I DO, THAT THIS CARNAGE WILL SOON BECOME A PART OF HIS LEGEND. AND EVEN IF THE IMPERIAL ARMY MANAGES TO GET THROUGH... EVEN IF THE COSSACKS FAIL TO SURROUND US... IN TWO CENTURIES, THE NAME OF THIS RIVER WILL BE SYNONYMOUS WITH FAILURE. BEREZINA, THE SYMBOL OF DEFEAT.

OH YES, IN TWO CENTURIES' TIME, **EVERYBODY** WILL REMEMBER THIS DAY...
...BUT ONLY **I** WILL HAVE **LIVED** THROUGH IT.

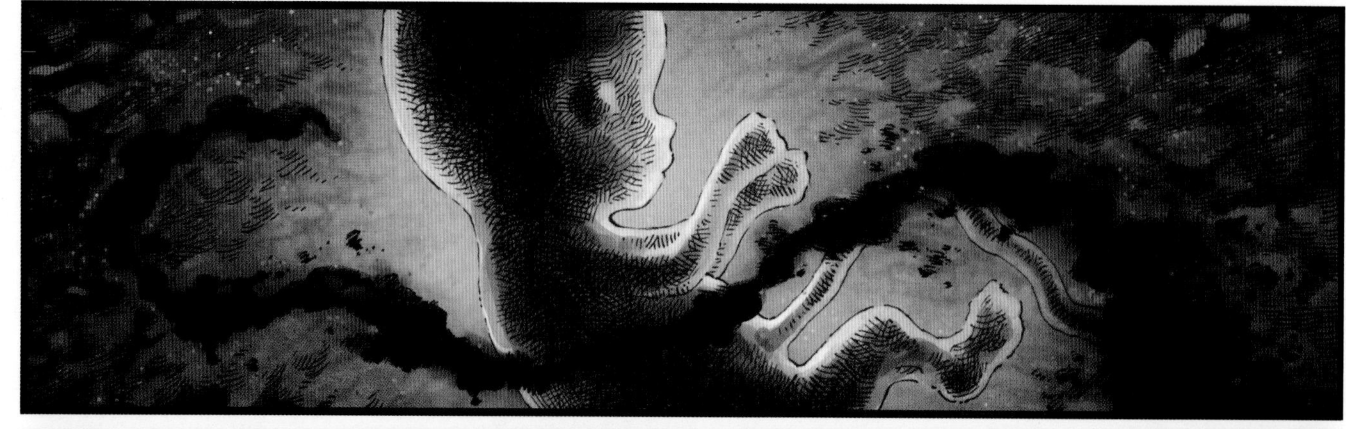

NO!

NO! NO, HE CAN'T! HE MUSTN'T...

KHOLYA, WAKE UP!
WE HAVE TO LEAVE NOW. GET THE OTHERS -- STERN, HARTMANN, FERAUD. TAKE FOOD AND AMMUNITION. PICK YOUR HORSES WELL -- WE'LL BE TRAVELLING FOR A LONG TIME...

...THEN MEET ME WHERE THE HORSES SLEEP.

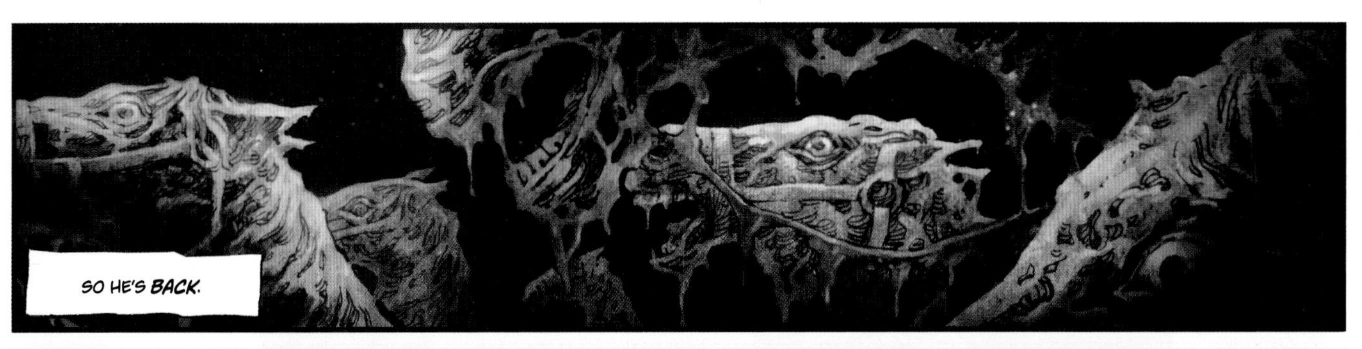
SO HE'S **BACK**.

I LEFT HIM, ALMOST THREE CENTURIES AGO, IN THE **JUNGLES** OF THE NEW WORLD... BUT HE CAME BACK. MY **BROTHER**. AND WHAT HE'S DONE NOW... HE'S COMMITTED THE **WORST** CRIME OF ALL.

THERE'S NO TIME TO WASTE... I MUST FIND RADU, AND **FINISH** THIS.

I HATE THIS PLACE. THOSE HORSES REALLY GIVE ME THE CREEPS... WHY ARE WE HERE, CAPTAIN?
A NEW MISSION? WE GONNA SERVE AS MESSENGERS? ARE WE GOING BACK TO PARIS?
BE QUIET, LADS... ALLOW THE CAPTAIN TO EXPLAIN.

IT'S SIMPLE, BOYS. WE'RE GOING TO DESERT.

I'VE SEEN EVERYTHING THERE IS TO SEE IN THIS CAMPAIGN. WHY SLAVE AWAY IN THE LOSING CAMP?

IF WE CONTINUE FIGHTING FOR THE EMPEROR, THE WINTER WILL CLOSE IN UPON US. JUST LIKE THE ICE TRAPPED THOSE POOR HORSES...

SO WE'RE GOING OVER TO THE OTHER SIDE? WE'RE GONNA FIGHT FOR THE RUSSIANS NOW?

NO. WE'RE GOING ON A TRIP.
A TRIP? WHERE?
TO THE WALLACHIAN MOUNTAINS. TWO WEEKS FROM HERE ON HORSEBACK....

WHAT THE HELL ARE WE GONNA DO THERE? DO THEY HAVE AN ARMY STATIONED THERE OR SOMETHING? ARE THEY HIRING?

NO. WE'VE GONE THROUGH ENOUGH 'HELL; AT SOMEONE ELSE'S BEHEST. INSTEAD WE WILL GO SEARCHING FOR A FORTUNE. THE WAR TREASURE OF AN ANCIENT TYRANT, WHOSE REPUTATION IN HIS TIME WAS EVEN GREATER THAN OUR EMPEROR'S...

...WE'RE GOING TO LOOK FOR VLAD DRACULA TEPES'S LOST TREASURE.

THEY BELIEVED ME, OF COURSE.

IT DID TAKE SOME TIME, THOUGH. AND I HAD TO MAKE UP SOME NICE STORIES WITH PLENTY OF DETAILS... LIKE THE ONE I SAID I HEARD FROM A GYPSY, RIGHT AFTER THE RAID OF SMOLENSK...

...THE ONE ABOUT MY FAMOUS KNIFE, WHICH REALLY DID BELONG TO VLAD TEPES... AND, IN FACT, STILL DOES.

AS FOR THE TREASURE, I'M QUITE CERTAIN, OF COURSE, THAT WE WON'T FIND IT. BUT I'LL NEED THESE MEN TO HELP ME IN MY QUEST...

...IT WILL TAKE ALL OF US TO DEFEAT MY BROTHER.

EAT -- DRINK
-- FUCK -- SLEEP
-- EAT -- DRINK
-- FUCK -- SLEEP
-- EAT...

THINK -- NO -- TOO HARD
-- THINK -- YES -- I --
MUST -- THINK -- HUNGRY
-- I'M -- HUNGRY...

EAT.
DRINK.
FUCK.
SLEEP.

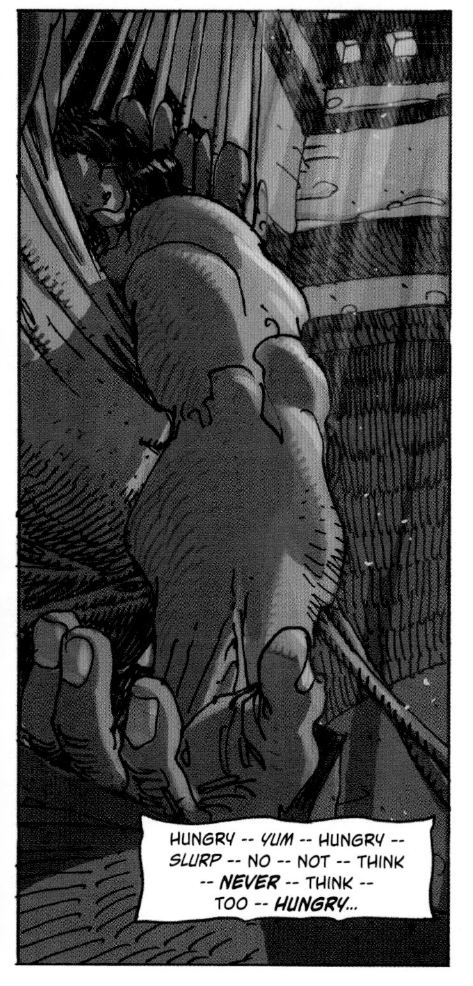
HUNGRY -- YUM -- HUNGRY --
SLURP -- NO -- NOT -- THINK
-- NEVER -- THINK --
TOO -- HUNGRY...

OUCH!

OH -- YES -- THIS -- BLOOD -- ALL -- THIS - BLOOD -- - FOR -- ME -- MORE...

I'M SWIMMING. I'M SPEEDING UP. I'M FLOATING. I'M MULTIPLYING AND I'M THINKING...

...AGAIN... I'M THINKING!

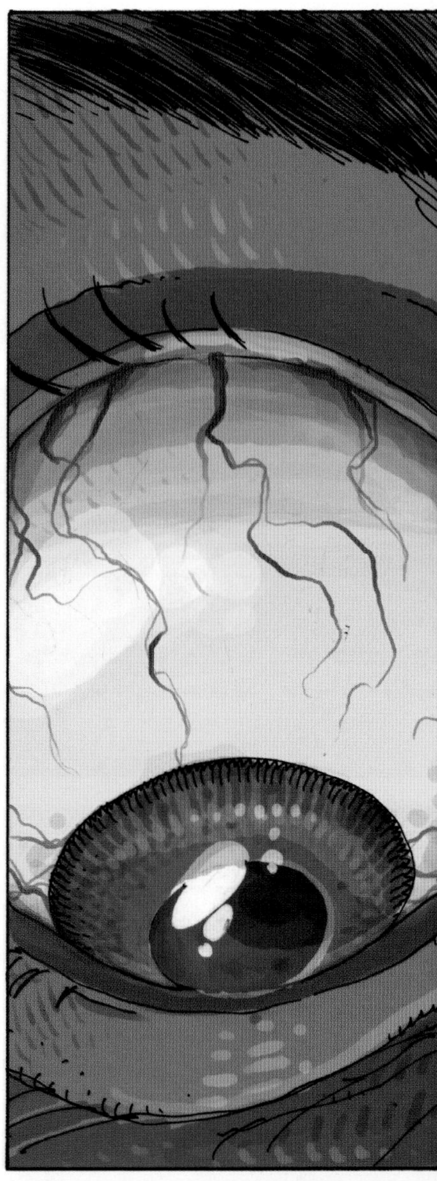

I... I AM A MAN AGAIN... I AM A SAILOR... OH YES... IT FEELS SO GOOD TO REMEMBER...

I AM MYSELF AGAIN... I AM... RADU!

I'M SAILING... BUT WHERE *TO*? I'M LIVING... BUT *WHEN*?

I NEED ANSWERS, IMAGES... NEED TO PUT THESE MEMORIES THAT ARE NOT MINE IN ORDER... *THERE*! THAT'S IT!

CRISTIANO PUERTA! THAT'S MY NAME! I GOT ON BOARD IN CADIZ... I HAVE A WIFE, CHILDREN... *NO!* WHO CARES! THAT'S *NOT* WHAT I NEED.

I NEED TO KNOW THE YEAR.... WHICH YEAR?

1509.

Webster & Associates

London, april 27th 1887

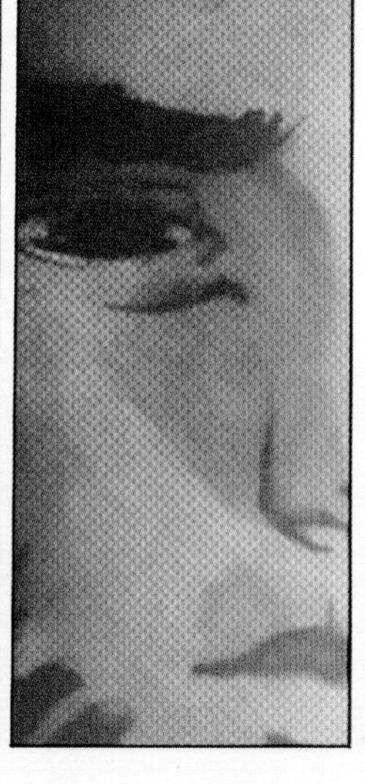

Following your instructions, we have meticulously investigated Victor Douglas Thorpe's life.

After studying law at Cambridge, Victor Douglas Thorpe was hired by our competitors, Fairywell, Cornwall & Wells, as a lowly clerk.

He's been languishing there for four years now, without any hope of ever making partner.

Thorpe lives alone, in a furnished flat on Lark Street, close to the disreputable Whitechapel area. He has no close friends and does not socialize with his colleagues.

His former classmates describe him as 'intelligent, but so reserved, as to seem almost aloof'.

CLAK
CLAK
CLAK
CLAK
'Discreet', 'unremarkable' even, are the words most often used about him by his colleagues and neighbors.

Only a certain Miss Esther Harrington, employed as secretary at Fairywell, Cornwall & Wells, seems close to him…

Victor Thorpe has paid numerous visits to Miss Harrington's home over the last few weeks.

He occasionally spends the night there.

"VICTOR ?"

GO BACK TO SLEEP, ESTHER.

HOW MUCH DO YOU NEED, VICTOR?

IT.. IT'S NOT WHAT YOU THINK... I WAS JUST LOOKING FOR...

HOW MUCH?

WHO DO YOU THINK I AM? I'M NOT A THIEF!

I... I'M SORRY, VICTOR. I DIDN'T MEAN TO MAKE YOU UNCOMFORTABLE.
REALLY? WELL, YOU MANAGED TO DO JUST THAT.

WAIT, VICTOR... I... I'M SORRY...
CLAK
I HAVE TO GO HOME... I NEED TO GET CHANGED. I'LL SEE YOU AT THE OFFICE.

Furthermore, Miss Harrington's repeated visits to Doctor Harry Niles, of Ashley Road, have aroused our interest.

For a small fee, Doctor Niles kindly confirmed what we suspected...

...Miss Harrington is pregnant.

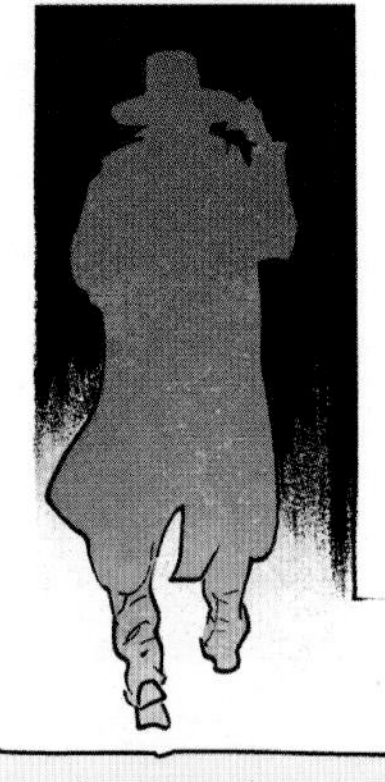
She is anxiously waiting for Victor Thorpe to ask her to marry him, but the latter seems to be in no hurry to do so...

...It can be safely assumed that he's ignoring Miss Harrington's condition.

Victor Thorpe is clearly addicted to gambling.
Due to this habit, his lifestyle far exceeds his financial means, and he is heavily indebted to certain Whitechapel usurers.
A rather unsavory character named Hathaway apparently has in his possession a promisory note signed by Victor Thorpe for a sum in excess of £3000.

Knowing the habits of the Whitechapel money lenders and similar gambling den owners. .

. . .we can safely assume that, unless his financial situation changes soon to allow him to settle his debts. . .

. . .the days of Victor Douglas Thorpe are numbered.

Consequently, it seems that this individual's profile fits your expectations in all respects: a young man from a good family, solitary, with no future.

I await your confirmation to make contact with him.
Yours respectfully,
Morris Webster

THERE'S A LETTER FOR YOU.
AH, THANKS.
MAYBE IT'S A JOB OFFER...
WELL?
IT'S AN INVITATION TO THE OPERA.
THE OPERA?
FOR ONE.

VICTOR DOUGLAS THORPE? MORRIS WEBSTER. AT YOUR SERVICE.
MORRIS WEBSTER? OF WEBSTER & ASSOCIATES?
IN THE FLESH. PLEASE TAKE A SEAT. THE PERFORMANCE IS JUST ABOUT TO START.
IT'S A GREAT HONOR TO MEET YOU, SIR! I WROTE TO YOU ON 19TH FEBRUARY TO APPLY FOR A JOB...
RE NOT INTERESTED.
HERE, TAKE MY BINOCULARS. LOOK AT THE BOX OPPOSITE US, IN THE TOP TIER. THE THIRD FROM THE RIGHT.

THE LIGHT IS OFF. I CAN'T SEE ANYONE...
NATURALLY. IF YOU COULD SEE HIM, YOU'D BE THE FIRST PERSON IN OVER THIRTY YEARS TO BEHOLD LORD BYRON CAVENDISH...
LORD CAVENDISH? HE'S HERE?
YES, MR THORPE. HE LEFT HIS MANSION FOR THE FIRST TIME SINCE THE CROWNING OF QUEEN VICTORIA...
...AND HE CAME TO SEE YOU.
M...ME? LORD CAVENDISH KNOWS ME? BUT THAT'S... THAT'S IMPOSSIBLE! HE'S THE RICHEST MAN IN THE EMPIRE, AND I... I'M NO ONE!
THAT'S CORRECT. YOU ARE NO ONE. WE HAVE MADE INQUIRIES ABOUT YOU... AND THAT'S EXACTLY THE CONCLUSION AT WHICH WE HAVE ARRIVED.
AS FOR THE JOB THAT LORD CAVENDISH HAS FOR YOU, YOU WILL FIND THE DETAILS IN THIS LETTER. AS I'M NOT AWARE OF ITS CONTENTS, I REQUEST THAT YOU WAIT UNTIL I'VE LEFT BEFORE OPENING IT.
AS A LAWYER, I BELIEVE IT'S OFTEN BEST NOT TO KNOW MORE THAN IS NECESSARY... I BID YOU A GOOD EVENING, MR THORPE.

WAIT! YOU... YOU COULD AT LEAST TELL ME WHY I WAS CHOSEN!
HE LIKED YOUR INITIALS.
KRiiiip
My last will and testament, by Lord Byron Cavendish

Víctor Douglas Thorpe,
As my sole heir...

TO BE CONTINUED...